What Readers and Critics say about the Poetry of Felix Dennis

"This is marvellous stuff... a 21st century Kipling. He rollicks and rolls with rhyme, meter, and melody."

— **Tom Wolfe**, *critic and author*

"He writes like a man obsessed... If Waugh were still alive, he would fall on Dennis's verse with a glad cry of recognition and approval."

— **John Walsh**, *The Independent*

"It is so rare one comes across a modern poet whose talent leaps off of every page and who has had the good grace to respect poetry by using rhyme, paying attention to cadence, and, at the same time, so involving you in each poem, you forget these necessary structures. Not since the Welsh poet-magician, Dylan Thomas, has a British poet seemed so well poised to gain a wide audience..."

— **Alan Caruba**, *Editor, bookviews.com*

"*A Glass Half Full* is funny, poignant and a breath of fresh air."

— **Sarah Broadhurst**, *The Bookseller*

"Great quality and memorability. At least one of these poems will be instantly anthologised."

— **Melvyn Bragg**, *broadcaster and author*

"What a total, utter joy to receive a copy of Felix Dennis's latest collection of poetry... almost guaranteed to be one of the biggest-selling books of new poetry in the UK. He gives us a volume packed with unpretentious poems drawn largely from his own life, experiences and observations — this is what makes them so real, so readable and, above all, so enjoyable."

— **Richard Fair**, *bbc.co.uk*

"I enjoy his poetry immensely."

— **Mick Jagger**, *singer, songwriter*

"...an engaging monster, filled with contradictions and reeking of sulphur."

— **The Times**

"Dennis confronts issues ranging from the holocaust to Elvis with equal poetic and emotional skill. The verse sweeps from darkly poignant to hilariously funny."

— **John Severs**, *Ottakar's New Title Reviews*

"I enjoyed *A Glass Half Full* more than I can possibly say. Brilliant!"

— **Helen Gurley Brown**, *Editor in Chief, Cosmopolitan*

"A fantastic collection! Rich, sumptuous and beautifully threaded."

— **Jon Snow**, *Channel 4 broadcaster*

"A knockout! Full of wisdom, compassion, humour and worldly insight."

— **Richard Neville**, *author and broadcaster*

"I don't think I have ever known such a sense of celebration and occasion in all of the years of our poetry programme. You feel he lived it so richly, so dangerously, so that he could be so wise for our delight"

— **Dr. Robert Woof**, *Director of The Wordsworth Trust*

"Serious, witty, thought provoking and moving. You may even cry! I loved it."

— **Dave Reynolds**, *Radio Warwick*

"I don't know which is better: hearing [him] read them aloud or reading the book itself. Deftly amusing on first hearing, his verse repays much closer inspection."

— **Dotun Adebayo**, *BBC Radio London*

"*A Glass Half Full* is the poetry of real life... the power to raise a smile in one who never laughs; to wring tears from another who hasn't wept since kindergarten; and to bring a measure of consolation to the inconsolable."

— **Anita Lafford**, *sculptor*

"The way poetry should be. The sort of book that can make poetry popular again."

— **Alex Frankel**, *amazon.co.uk*

"...ingeniously executed, impishly absurd, wryly insightful."

— **Heidi Dawlet**, *Media Life*

"Felix is a pirate and a passionate poet... an evening to remember."

— **Michael Boyd**, *Artistic Director, Royal Shakespeare Company*

"Many people were deeply moved by the humanity of his verse and by the range of his experience [in these] haunting poems."

— **Tom Wujec**, *TED (Technology, Entertainment &Design) Conference, Monterey, California*

"An unforgettable evening... to hear him perform was awe-inspiring."

— **Sandy Holt,**
The Stratford-upon-Avon Herald

"Those of you who missed Felix Dennis at his UK-wide tour appearances should weep. By the fourth poem he had the audience drinking out of his hand."

— **Don Barnard,** *Reviews Gate.com*

"One can recreate the visual image so clearly – hearing, sense of touch, sense of smell – they are so evocative in his poetry. It's enthralling."

— **Isobel Yule,**
National Library for the Blind

"Dennis is a literary star in his own right. He makes it look easy – damn him! I couldn't put the book down. Just one question remains: what took Dennis so long to come out as a poet? And are there more where these came from? God, I hope so!"

— **Z. Menthos,** *critic.org*

"Felix Dennis is a poet of the Hemingway, Kipling, Frost or even Rod McKuen variety... It will not take long for the world to realize his genius and voice. His poetry is that good."

— **Claudia VanLydegraf,** *myshelf.com*

"*A Glass Half Full* contains the best poetry in decades."

— **Jed Pressgrove,** *The Reflector,*
College Publisher Network

"A one of a kind book. Some poems [are] delicious, deeply sensitive and serious; others [are] humorous, even bawdy. For poetry lovers with a liking for dry humor and much wit... I highly recommend it. Five stars."

— **Elizabeth R. Mastin,** *amazon.com*

"I was enticed along to an evening of Felix Dennis's poetry by the promise of free wine, but in all honesty I would happily pay to see him again and again! If all poetry was written with the same passion, humour and senses of nostalgia and morality as this, then poetry would once again be one of the foremost art forms in this country."

— **Martin G. Bryant,** *amazon.co.uk*

"Felix Dennis gives us poetry with roots in the 60s and a 21st century relevance. I could rave on, but I won't. Get your own copy and settle down with a glass of vino — you have hours of enjoyment ahead."

— **Hilary Williamson,** *bookloons.com*

ISLAND
Of DREAMS

99 Poems from Mustique

To Andreas and Catherine Heeschen
with kindest regards,

Felix Dennis

By the Same Author

A Glass Half Full
(Hutchinson) 2002

Lone Wolf
(Hutchinson) 2004

The Taking of Saddam:
A Ballad
(Noctua Press) 2004

When Jack Sued Jill:
Nursery Rhymes for Modern Times
(Ebury Press) 2006

and coming in 2008
Homeless in My Heart

NOCTUA PRESS
Set in Sabon and Univers

All titles available on Amazon or at other good booksellers
or from **www.felixdennis.com**

www.felixdennis.com
also contains many poems, published and unpublished,
as well as a library of sound recordings and video footage
of Felix Dennis's verse and poetry tours.
Not for the faint of heart!

Felix Dennis

ISLAND *of* DREAMS

99 Poems from Mustique

Photography by Sybil Sparkes

Designed by Rebecca Jezzard · Illustrations by Bill Sanderson

NOCTUA PRESS

First published by Noctua Press 2007

Noctua Press
9 - 11 Kingly Street
London W1B 5PN
ISBN 978-0-9528385-3-1

Designed by Rebecca Jezzard
Illustrations by Bill Sanderson
Photography by Sybil Sparkes
Printed and bound by Butler & Tanner Ltd

Copies of this book may be purchased from:

The Mustique Company offices

The Mustique Community Library

Retail outlets, boutiques, bars, restaurants and
the hotel and guest house on Mustique

Noctua Press
islandofdreams@dennis.co.uk

www.felixdennis.com

www.amazon.co.uk

Single copies: US$25.00 per copy
Six copies or more: US$20 per copy

For the Hon. Brian Alexander
who stayed the course
and got it done

'The history of all human ideas
is a history of irresponsible dreams.'
— **Sir Karl Popper**

Foreword

Island of Dreams is a very small token of my appreciation towards the people of St. Vincent and the Grenadines, together with the inhabitants and homeowners of a tiny island measuring just three miles by one. An island called Mustique.

Nearly all the poems in this book were written on Mustique. Sybil Sparkes's wonderful photographs accompanying them were taken there, too.

Some of the poems are concerned with life on the island, as seen through the eyes of a transplanted semi-resident. Others attempt a wider canvas, but are indelibly coloured (for their author, at least) by the atmosphere of an endlessly fascinating pinprick, a microcosm if you will, of humanity — rich and poor, mogul and fisherman, local and yachtie, worker and villa-renter — all to be found sharing 'an emerald set in a turquoise sea'.

Mustique's Lilliputian environment, climate, geography, flora and fauna have also played their part in the writing of these poems. Sky and sea, especially, are ever present. They invade the mind, casting a spell that serves to mock everyday cares and human self-importance, bringing with them a sense of unreality, an uncertainty that the outside world exists at all. Or so it seems to me.

To some, Mustique is known as little more than a playground for the rich and the famous. But I believe it represents something rather more profound. In my view, today's Mustique is a unique social, cooperative experiment; one which began as a stylish house party and which is now maturing into a cohesive community.

I was made welcome on Mustique by innumerable people from the moment my feet touched the tarmac of 'an airport built of bamboo' thirteen years ago. Unfailing kindness, a sense of wry mischief, tolerance and good humour are infectious.

How lucky Marie-France and I were to find our way here, to this island of dreams.

— Felix Dennis

Mandalay, Mustique
September, 2007

'The flowers of desire…'

The flowers of desire from our youth,
    (Those thistle seeds of waking and obsession),
Lie scattered by the harvesters of truth,
    And perish in the winter of possession.

FEBRUARY, 2004

Night Lilies on Mustique

Our tropic flowers, brash and bright,
Have shut their gaudy for the night,
And only lilies bloom.

White lilies, with their drooping fronds
And sickly sheen, swim in the ponds:
Moth-baiters in the gloom.

No bud or petal flaunts its glow
For men— though we may think it so
And tend them in our plot,

And sweat to show green-fingered skill
In bending nature to our will:
Yet who bends which to what?

For are not men mere moths who sow,
Who weed and water, prick and grow
That blossom, or this grass?

Who bottle-up their heady scents;
Who build them costly monuments
In palaces of glass?

The flowers were here before we came;
You think that we have bred them tame
And it was ever thus?

Yet men it was who raised and hurled
Their stranded seed across the world:
The *flowers* it was, tamed *us!*

And tamed us well. As men trick bees,
They awed us with their mysteries
Of colour and perfume.

Our tropic flowers, brash and bright,
Have shut their gaudy for the night,
And only lilies bloom.

FEBRUARY, 2006

On Entering My New 'Writer's Cottage' On Mustique For The First Time

Here in a fastness, filled with light
In view of a turquoise sea,
A fool has banished himself to write,
And, oh! that fool is me.

Here where the moon lies on her back
Beneath a star-struck dome,
Where planet and star have lost their track,
Where crab and turtle roam;

Here is the balm when force had failed,
When craft and wit run out;
The turn of the tide for hopes derailed
In lands of weary doubt;

Here in a haven, purpose built,
With hills on either side,
I banish the cares of coin and guilt
And cast excuse aside;

Here where the wind is soft and South,
Behind a slatted blind,
A fool may learn to stop his mouth
And search his heart and mind.

And what he shall find, the sages knew
From Aristotle down:
That his mind contains in Xanadu
What it did in London town.

DECEMBER, 2004

9

Of Paradise

If it were left to men or mice
To conjure their own paradise—
If elephant or witless flea
Were masters of eternity—
What fool would wish to wake each day
Where tigers hunt undying prey,
Or in a world where Fat Joe scoffs
His cakes in everlasting troughs,
Where Bogie struts in black and white
Through Casablanca every night,
Or worse, where adolescence reigns
And spotters tick off deathless trains
While virgins bearing ice-cold beer
Sing sweet endearments in their ear?
If it were left to such as these,
To mice or men or witless fleas,
Then we should learn, perhaps too well,
The truest measurement— of hell,
Where one man's fantasy of wit
For others, emulates the pit.

10

AUGUST, 2004

The Garden of Life

Our lives are less a journey than a garden
Of virgin soil, inherited at birth;
And none but fools would covet, still less pardon,
The motley plants we nourish in its earth.

The bitter fruit of malice and rejection,
The ivy of despair that cloaks a wall,
Tall shrubs of pride, so sure of their perfection,
(Their scabby leaves a wilderness of gall);

And here, a single rose: an act of kindness,
Unsullied by the fungal blight of gain;
But see— the nettles, representing blindness
To any other's misery or pain;

And here, the saddest sight: a child's sapling
Stunted in its yearning for the light,
While overhead, dark mistletoe is grappling
With leprous moss as envy succours spite.

And here, a bed of honesty and honour,
(Surprising, is it not, to find it here?
Still, men are all half whore, and half Madonna;)
This evil copse is nightmare grown to fear.

The sapling? Were it walnut we could whip it,
The ivy will destroy it if it can;
Yet given light, the sapling will outstrip it,
The Tree of Hope was God's last gift to man.

MARCH, 2006

'An elephant carries the world on his back...'

An elephant carries the world on his back,
He carries it far, he carries it back,
He swings to the left, he swings to the right,
And the ants on the ball call it morning and night.

An elephant carries the world on his back,
With his trumpeting, seas and continents crack,
When he circles the sun on his shadowy wing
The ants on the ball call it winter or spring.

An elephant carries the world on his back,
His tongue is a sunset of ruin and wrack,
When he waggles an ear there is storm or typhoon,
And the ants on the ball think his eye is the moon.

An elephant carries the world on his back,
And once in a while his saddle grows slack,
And sometimes he swallows a star with a sneeze
As the ants on the ball tumble down on their knees.

An elephant carries the world on his back,
He carries it far, he carries it back,
His trunk is the source of the rain and the mist—
But the ants on the ball say he doesn't exist!

FEBRUARY, 2006

Christmas Eve in the Tropics

No snow, no mistletoe, no tolling bell;
The tropic moon is polished to a gem.
So strange— and yet what snowflake ever fell
On Joseph's wife and child in Bethlehem?

DECEMBER, 2001

The Man Who Built Mustique

[In Memoriam: Arne Hasselqvist]

Half saint, half sinner — and all buccaneer,
I'll sing you the ballad of a bold pioneer,
A man with a plan and the devil's cheek;
      This was the man who built Mustique.

Way back when the lots were sticks in the sand,
It was Arne who mapped and plotted and planned
A paradise built from stone and teak.
      This was the man who built Mustique.

He could build 'em big, he could build 'em small,
He could build you a palace or a hole-in-the-wall,
And each one 'finished by Christmas week!'
      This was the man who built Mustique.

He built for the lords and he built for the fools,
He built with his hands when there *were* no tools,
Each was a monument, each unique;
      This was the man who built Mustique.

With his last brick laid and a life's work done,
Arne's blue-print epitaphs stand in the sun;
If roofs could talk or the walls could speak…
      This was the man who built Mustique!

FEBRUARY, 2001

17

Arne Hasselqvist arrived in St.Vincent and the Grenadines from his native Sweden with his wife Anita during the mid 1960's. Eventually, in 1968, he was invited to Mustique by Hugo Money-Coutts, the managing director of the island which was at that time owned by Colin Tennant. Labouring under utterly primitive conditions, Arne began transforming Colin's tropical paradise dream into a breathtaking architectural reality. By the turn of the century Arne had played a major part in constructing the Cotton House Hotel, the Mustique Primary School, the original Basil's Bar, bunk houses for his workers, a building yard, an airport, various shops and stores and miles of service roads. In addition, he designed and construct 55 spectacular homes for some of the most demanding clients in the world. His sales technique towards prospective buyers was legendary, and inevitably concluded with the triumphant clincher: "… and it will <u>all</u> be finished by Christmas week!" What Arne did not specify was <u>which</u> Christmas he had in mind. He was a remarkable man who brought skills and employment to hundreds of Vincentians. His tragic death, along with his son Lukas, in a fire on Grand Bahama Island in 2001, saddened us all. To say that Arne Hasselqvist was the man who built Mustique is not poetic licence — it is the simple truth.

On the Rights & Wrongs of Custom

When custom preaches: *'This was not thought wrong'*,
    You may be sure the thought protects the strong:
What reason lacks, then passion must supply—
    Though Time will bring more converts than the Lie.

MARCH, 2005

*With a solemn tip of the hat
to that true hero and friend of
the common man, Tom Paine.*

'Nother Day in Paradise

Basil's having breakfast, Ali's baking bread,
Frank is at the harbour, rhyming in his head,
Eddie's by the taxi, leaning in the sun,
'Nother day in Paradise, brother, just begun.

Teacher checking homework, Kurt checking notes,
Someone in the pasture checking on the goats,
Bev's checking money, Ken's checked a fool,
Ladies checking libr'ry shelves by the school.

Samson got a cylinder swung down a rung,
Doctor's in his surgery — peering at a tongue,
Stable's combing ponies, Lotty's on design,
Peter's fixing generators, Stan's tasting wine.

Fish are in the market flopping on the block,
Ferry boat container clogging up the dock,
Jeremiah's sweeping, Patrick's stacking beer,
Sweaty work in Paradise— wish you were here!

Quartermaster tongue-lashing down at the camp,
Trailer's tipped a power boat down at the ramp,
Diane at a reef ball, coach at the net,
Things here are humming but we ain't done yet.

Toby on a Segway rolling down the hill,
Brian selling real estate — 'nother ten mill',
Pippa's in the pantry, Karen's on the go,
(She won't tell you nothin' you don't need t'know).

Johanna's on the tel'phone ordering a dress,
Thomas on a blueprint calculating stress,
Liz is busy jogging, Tony's on site:
'Brother, where's your hard hat? Do the job right.'

Stephen's at the Company balancing the books,
Keeping track of coin be harder than it looks,
Lavinia and Lou both busier'n bees,
Hamlet on the pumps and Ronnie on his knees.

Val is at the paperwork, juggling dates,
Down at the supermarket— *'Mind them crates!'*
Depot got delivery— battery's flat.
Wayne's got a wrench out: "Le'me fix that."

Queues at the airport, George in the tower,
Jonathan revving on a bitty plane's power,
Waiting on a non-sched'— ain't come yet:
Brother, mind your language: *'Hi there, Jeannette.'*

Villa-renters barbecuing down at the beach,
Solly on a septic: "Can't let it leach."
Sniggers in the bushes — weedy kinda cough:
'And here's Mr. Adams, so you better knock it off!'

Fishing in the channel using Darnley's bait,
Reeling in a big one. Getting kind of late.
Cold rum and coke and a fat, pink sun,
'Nother day in Paradise— done, brother, done.

SEPTEMBER, 2007

Sonnet for H20

[For Loren Eiseley]

Strange how the spark of life stirs not in fire,
Nor air, nor earth, but swims in viscous ooze
And shallow brine, its alchemy a weeping fuse
Of slime, a reeking womb propelled entire
By water. Water from a toxic mire,
From snowflakes, foaming brooks and morning dews,
From estuaries feeding silent deeps,
From marsh and mist and noon-dark monsoon rains.
Into the planet's molten heart, through veins
Of scoured rock and ice, earth's water creeps
And drips, and trickles, leaches, drains and seeps
Until, at last, past cave-blind fish, it gains
Once more the living Maine. And from some pool
Of warm, primaeval silt — produced this fool.

MAY, 2001

Loren Eiseley, for me the only scientist who ever wrote in a poet's tongue entire, deserves a far better sonnet than this. Sadly, it is the best that I can offer as my personal and sincere tribute to his memory. 'The Flow of the River' from his wonderful book *The Immense Journey* contains all the seeds of the above in prose that beggars description and shames my emulation. W.H. Auden in the *New Yorker* wrote of Eiseley: "I have eagerly read anything of his I could lay my hands on." So have I. And so should you, perhaps, whoever you are and whatever you do. Apart from *The Immense Journey*, I would also heartily recommend *The Star Thrower, The Unexpected Universe* and his stab at an autobiography, *All The Strange Hours*. Magical stuff! Nations and individuals who complain of America's global cultural dominance (often unearned in their opinion) would take heart from Eiseley.

The King of Mandalay

They told me, dear old Turbo, they told me you had died;
'The king be dead,' is what they said. I very nearly cried.
We'd had our disputations, our ups and downs, it's true —
But you were *the* most handsome cat I think I ever knew.

Those tiger, tiger markings; the eyes that burned so bright;
A layabout by daylight — a predator by night.
You bullied little Molly; your ways were rough and rude;
You never wanted petting — you always wanted food.

You'd loll among the pillows on some forbidden bed,
Or while away a sunny afternoon sprawled on my head;
But now the house feels empty and Molly seems to say:
"Oh where is my tormentor, Turbo — King of Mandalay?"

DECEMBER, 2000

Turbo was the tomcat at my home, 'Mandalay' in Mustique. I inherited him from
David Bowie. An extraordinarily handsome cat with tiger-stripe markings and
pronounced shoulder haunches, Turbo's walk was compared by many visitors to
that of a cheetah or a leopard. Foolhardy in the extreme, he constantly needed
the vet's attention because of his habit of fighting creatures stronger or larger than
himself. On several occasions, Turbo learned to get on the ferry at the dock and
take a trip to St. Vincent. He never left the ship until it returned to Mustique when
the harbour master would alert us and we would collect him. Molly is Mandalay's
lap cat, a petite white female. Turbo hated her with an abiding passion and
I was forced to throw him in the fish pond once or twice to teach him to mind
his manners. It was Tony, our old butler, who christened Turbo 'The King of
Mandalay', as indeed he was, but I never did find out why he was called Turbo in
the first place. The first line and the metre of *The King of Mandalay* is based on
William Johnson Cory's translation of *Heraclitus*.

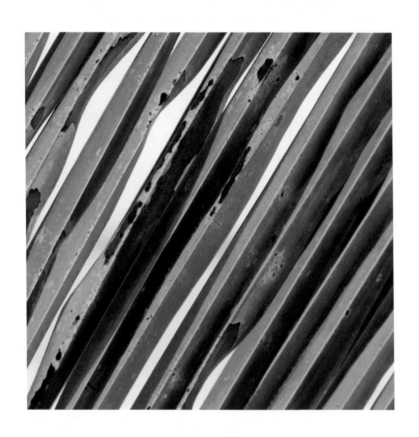

The Perilous Feast

I watched a red-legged tortoise,
    (Whose legs aren't 'red' at all)
Come lumbering down the terraces
    Beyond our garden wall.

The sodden scree was perilous
    Along the hanging tracks,
Especially for greedy-guts
    With homes upon their backs.

Her scaly limbs were balanced
    On stone as sharp as knives;
Yet on she came, oblivious,
    Her eyes fixed on the prize.

So close to turning turtle,
    That stubborn, ancient beast,
Risked death for one hibiscus flower,
    And then began her feast!

DECEMBER, 2000

Sunset, Mustique

A ball of fire is spilling in the sea,
The empty sky flamingo-pink and grey,
Cicada songs creak out the end of day,
A choir of tree-frogs whistle: 'Come to me!'

Our feral cat is sprawled upon the wall,
The stone still warm beneath her mottled fur;
Her lantern-green eyes blink — she will not stir
Until her food is brought, nor heed my call.

I sit upon a driftwood bench and stare,
The house is full of laughter, guests and light,
I dare not stay here long, hid in the night.
The bats are out! There's one... another there!

Some fool has rung the gong. I catch my breath
As suddenly I know that I've grown old,
The courtyard cobbles, lit with bars of gold,
Spell out the hieroglyphics of a death.

APRIL, 2004

This is the Song

This is the song that none can sing,
This is the gift the old gods bring,
Sung this once as the soul takes wing
In the emptiness of night.

Here is the powerlessness of speech,
The letting go that none can teach,
The song of things beyond our reach,
Singing to its own light.

APRIL, 2007

'We have no rights...'

We have no rights— except those born in tears;
And blood; and sweat; the bitter fruit of battle,
The gnawing at the heart of martyr's fears
Whose names we do not even know. The rattle
In their welling throats; the heel taps of the wracked;
Their screams as lumps of living flesh were tortured,
Burnt and scalded, dislocated, pierced and hacked
By Men of God— their masters in the orchard...
'My dear Archbishop, try another pear,
The cherry trees are sweeter by the chapel,
These heretics will soon repent, I swear.
Or would your Grace perhaps prefer an apple?'
    WE HAVE NO RIGHTS! but what we took by threat:
    They long to snatch them back, should we forget.

APRIL, 2004

'I built myself a house of wood...'

I built myself a house of wood
Where once an apple orchard stood.
On stormy nights I lay in bed
While rafters moaned above my head.

They wept aloud for limbs long lost,
For buds pinched out by early frost,
For wicker baskets piled with fruit,
For phantom branch and withered root.

I caulked the roof and rafter beams,
But still they whispered in my dreams,
They spoke of rising sap and wood:
— And then, at last, I understood.

This spring, I planted out a score
Of apple saplings by my door.
Now stormy nights my rafters chime
To cider choirs and nursery-rhyme.

MAY, 2003

Love Came to Visit Me

Love came to visit me,
 Shy as a fawn,
But finding me busy,
 She fled with the dawn.

At twenty, the torch of
Resentment was lit,
My rage at injustice
Waxed hot as the pit,
The flux of its lava
Cleared all in its path,
Comrades and enemies
Fled from its wrath.
Yet lovers grew wary
Once novelty waned —
To lie with a panther
Is terror unfeigned.

At thirty, my powers
Seemed mighty to me,
The fruits of my rivals
I shook from the tree,
By guile and by bluster,
By night and by day,
I battered and scattered
The fools from my way;
And women grew willing
To sham and to bluff —
Their trinkets and baubles
Cost little enough.

From forty to fifty,
Grown easy and sly
I wined 'em and dined 'em;
Like pigs in a sty
We feasted and revelled
And rutted in muck,
Forgetting our peril,
Forgetting to duck,
Forgetting time's arrows
Are sharper than knives,
Grown sick to our stomachs —
And sick of our lives.

Love came to visit me,
    Shy as a fawn,
But finding me busy,
    She fled with the dawn.

MARCH, 2002

Dementia

Lord, spare me from the emptiness of days,
From knowledge half remembered, half concealed;
From knowing winks that greet me in the maze,
From what lies in the pit— unshrived, unhealed.

Lord save me from the stench of bowel and tract,
From nurses with their hearty cries and broth,
From surgeons with their jargon and their tact,
Lord send me strength to vent a mighty wrath

Annihilating pity and its kind
From condescending fools who crowd my bed.
Lord grant me one clear day with clearer mind
In which to make my peace. Then strike me dead

Or send me one young grandson in his pride
In whose smooth face there shines my husband's wit;
Then I shall seek no further place to hide:
Just one clear day— and then fulfil Thy writ.

JANUARY, 2006

Love Letter

Late spring has kissed awake the walnut tree,
Snap dragons, wide-eyed lambs, the honey-bee,

Small rivers trailing blossom from the bough—
Yet you are all I seek of England now.

The land renews! — but not its mortal kind,
And we have left our springtimes far behind,

The snow is on our peaks, the creeks run dry;
I stare more at my feet than at the sky.

A life I've lived of laughter, aye, and pain,
A race that I would gladly run again,

But only with your gentle fingers pressed
To soothe this famished monster in my breast.

Soon now, I think, my spirit must depart,
And journey where I know not. Yet, dear heart,

If all impatient, first, your soul should steal,
Turn but your face — to find me at your heel!

MAY, 2003

For a pioneer Mustique homeowner and his
lovely wife who died within a short time of
each other following a last scuba dive together.

An Airport Built of Bamboo

for Barbara Deyell of 'Windsong')

We gathered ourselves at the airport,
(An airport built of bamboo),
The great and the good and the curious,
And those not sure it was true;
The doctor was there with his patient
And the mask of his face said it all,
(The tiny plane parked on the runway,
The customs, a hole in a wall);
And the dogs ran in circles around us
And the cats in their cages mewed,
And somebody pestered a helper,
Who answered with something rude,
And Barbara's maid was weeping,
And others began to cry,
And people around me grew hazy,
(I must have got grit in my eye),
And our big dog nuzzled my fingers,
And I somehow knew that he knew,
So I edged with him closer towards her,
And then didn't know what to do
Or to say, so I kissed her lightly,
While my big dog nudged her thigh,
And she patted his head and scratched him
With a nod and a watery eye;
And then, Marie-France and the ladies
And Stan and a dozen more,
Were saying there own 'get betters'
While most of us stared at the floor

Or stood by the fence with the pilot,
Who murmured, 'Make way there, please,'
(He's a good man is that pilot),
Then he gave my shoulder a squeeze
And led them out to the apron—
It was all going by in a blur—
Barbara, her pets and her daughter,
And I felt like a damn voyeur
As they lifted her into the cabin,
As gently as ever they could,
And I thought she mouthed, 'I'll see ya!'
(Though I knew that we never would),
And the pilot started the engines,
And somebody mumbled a prayer,
So I followed Jeannette and the others
Who were clambering up the stair
To the old, familiar platform,
Where we stood in a ragged line
And waved in the Mustique fashion,
As the engines grew from a whine
To a roar, and thundered towards us,
And she took to the sky like a bird;
Our arms dropped down from waving,
And nobody said a word,
As we shuffled across the concourse,
A solemn and silent crew
Who knew she was never returning
To an airport built of bamboo.

Word came a week or so later:
She had passed; but we shall not dwell
On her passing, for that is a journey
That none return to tell;
I know nothing of what comes after,
Nothing of heaven or God,
But I know that our old friend Barbara
Was Queen of the Awkward Squad;
She was tiny and brusque and clever,
And she cussed and was given to scold,
She never did suffer fools gladly,
But her heart was beaten gold;
And her frail frame hid a secret,
That beneath her crackling laugh,
There was kindness wrapped in a blanket,
And softness wrapped in chaff;
There was no better friend than Barbara,
As the luckiest of us knew,
When we gathered ourselves at the airport,
(An airport, built of bamboo).

FEBRUARY, 2006

Why I Write

For fame? I've drunk my fill of poisoned wells.
For coin? Five cents a word comes mighty cheap.
To taste that love of life which thought compels?
Aye, that: and so that others smile— or weep.

MARCH, 2005

The aim of an artist, Leo Tolstoy reflected in a letter to a friend, '...is not to resolve a question irrefutably but to compel one to love life in all its manifestations. If I were told that I could write a novel in which I could indisputably establish as true my point of view on all social questions, I would not dedicate two hours to such a work; but if I were told that what I wrote would be read twenty years from now by those who are children today, and that they would weep and laugh over it and fall in love with the life in it, then I would dedicate all my existence and all my powers to it.' Others may disagree with such an analysis— and, indeed, Tolstoy's point of view has never been a particularly popular one. Samuel Johnson insisted that 'no man but a blockhead ever wrote, except for money'. (If that were true, then Johnson's mighty labour upon his dictionary must have proved a poor investment.) But for sheer insight and unblinking honesty on the subject, Tolstoy, for me, comes closer to alembic perfection than anyone else I have read. Writing verse has helped me come to love life 'in all its manifestations', however inept my verse may be and however cynical and worldy-wise I was before I began. And yet, it is also undeniably true that I write in the hope I will be read by others. Poets like John Donne and Emily Dickinson, who published very little in their lifetime, are especially revered if they become popular posthumously— perhaps as much for holding true to a faith in their work, as for the merit of the work itself, however great.

Before— and After

When you're young— they want you older,
When you're old— they want you young;
When she's gone— you wish you'd told her,
When she's back— you bite your tongue.

When you're cross— its 'Let's not fight, dear,'
When you're tired— it's party time!
When you're hard— it's 'Not tonight, dear,'
When you're prose— she speaks in rhyme.

When you're broke— it's 'I've been thinking…'
When you're rich— it's '…join the gym!'
When you're ill— its '…all that drinking…'
When you're dead— it's 'Who? Oh, <u>him!</u>'

DECEMBER, 2003

Ol' Man Sorrow

Ol' Man Sorrow got a sack
Heavy 'nuff to break yo' back,

When you meet him on de road
Nebber, nebber share dat load,

Nod: "G'mornin' ", sidle by,
Cross yo'self and hope to die,

If he walk on — den you run!
Jumbie bad— he go to come!

If'en he chase af'er you
Get yo'self to Timbuktu,

If he follow, 'n he will,
Jump right out de win'owsill,

Sell yo' shoes and pawn yo' coat,
Smuggle yo'self 'board a boat,

If he vex you on de deck,
Tie de millstone roun' yo' neck,

Jump into de sea below —
Dat one place he *nebber* go.

JULY, 2001

'*When sorrows come, they come not single spies, / But in battalions.*' (Hamlet act 4, sc 5.)
In the West Indies, they come in a sack. The name and many of the lines from this sly
'nursery rhyme' came from a group of Bequia fisherman at their village on Mustique's
Britannia Bay over a 'boil-up' and several cups of rum. Political correctness probably
demands that 'de' be spelt as 'the'; 'yo' be spelt 'your' and 'nebber' be spelt 'never' etc.
But as my pc allegiance rating is zero, and as that is not how the words are pronounced,
I have spelt them as spoken. A 'jumbie' is an evil spirit or bogey man in these parts.

Caged Fire

I always had my way, as you had yours;
Each to the other courteous but firm,
Interpreters of verdicts, codes and laws,
Of jurisdiction, penalty and term,
Softening confrontation where we could—
Our love no less for that and no less rash
Than vulgar fires of paraffin and wood
That blaze a while and then subside to ash.
A widened eye served notice of dissent;
A slight embrace, apology in full;
A short 'Good night' to signal discontent;
Our bed the only site of push and pull.
    The world misunderstood such lack of show:
    Serenity without— caged fire below.

APRIL, 2006

An Old Dog Is The Best Dog

An old dog is the best dog,
A dog with rheumy eyes;
An old dog is the best dog
A dog grown sad and wise;
    Not one who snaps at bubbles,
      Nor one who barks at nowt —
        A dog who knows your troubles,
        A dog to see you out.

An old bitch is the best bitch,
Not pups to fetch your sticks;
An old bitch is the best bitch,
Not one to teach new tricks;
    Not one who's up and leaping,
      But one whose coat is grey —
        Leg's twitching while she's sleeping
        In dreams of yesterday.

AUGUST, 2001

The Children of Wood

Every age is a wood age, as it has been from the first,
A char-fired stick for a weapon— let nature do her worst;
We harried the squealing mammoth to pits of sharpened logs,
Roasting his flesh on wood fires, tossing a bone to our dogs.

From wood we smelted iron— and hollowed the first canoes,
Of wood we built our temples to banish our own taboos,
Wood fired the kilns of our potters, from bark we wove our twine
To fasten the first ship's rigging and fashion a fishing line.

On wood we rolled our heelstones across a downland moor,
Of wood we built the chariot wheels that filled the world with war,
On wood we first cut tallies, with wood new lines were drawn—
(Beside the walls of Babylon, geometry was born).

Then came the strangest birthing from an exiled eunuch's shame,
T'sai Lun invented paper, and the world was never the same,
What use our poets and writers, or the alphabets of men,
Without the pulp to spread the word? Wood had triumphed again!

➤

The beds of our trains were wooden, the pulleys that held our ropes,
The cross of the Christian saviour became the prop of Popes,
And the touch of a joiner's sanding or the grain of a carver's art
Still melts the hearts of monsters or warms a craftsman's heart.

Watch wood burn in a fireplace and the past returns, revealed,
When wood was our only ally, and fire our only shield,
We are wedded to wood as surely as a bole is wedded to bark—
So bless the trees, my children, they kept you from the dark;

They nurtured and they sustained us, they raised us from the dust,
It is time now, to repay them; in truth, we know we must,
Not just for their stately beauty, not just because we should—
We owe them more than duty: We are the children of wood!

AUGUST, 2007

'True coin — the finest armour...'

True coin — the finest armour ever wrought!
  With such as this I smote love in the dust
And conquered worlds; but now that time grows short,
  No smithy's art can free my heart of rust.

JULY, 2003

Conversation with a Leg

'So did you think great thoughts today, my dear?
    Now put away that nasty pipe and sit.'
He sat, removed a pencil from his ear
    And slipped away his only vice, unlit.

'No, no great thoughts! — but Bucky just came by.
    They granted us our patent.' 'Well, that's nice.'
She looked up from the bed and caught his eye:
    'Perhaps I'll take some snaps of paradise —

I'm dying, Albert. Get that in your head!
    Your silly toys can wait — until I've died.'
'I'm looking for a miracle,' he said.
    'The mirror is *behind* you,' she replied.

JANUARY, 2003

In the summer of 1936 Albert Einstein and his friend Dr. Gustav Bucky were granted patent No. 2050562 from the U.S. Patent Office for an 'automatic camera'. Einstein's second wife, Elsa, was already bedridden. She died a few months later. Their marriage had not been without difficulties but her loyalty to the great man was absolute. She worried constantly about his inability to deal with the 'real world' and generally treated the most outstanding intellect of the 20th century as a recalcitrant child. Following her death Einstein wrote to fellow scientist, Max Born: "I think I've lost a leg. It was a little crippled. I limped a bit on that leg, but I've still lost a leg."

Dancing Bees

Like dancing bees, we stumble from our hives
And bumble off in search of nectared fame;
A careless sting rips out our fumbling lives,
And worker, drone or Queen— we fare the same.

For what? For *what!* For honey in the sky?
For heaven's combs where bee-gods whir and dance
On endless summer days; where no bees die?
Dream on; the days grow short. The sting is chance.

DECEMBER, 2005

More

More them in the world than we.
More lock in the world than key.

More sky in the world than roof.
More why in the world than proof.

More dirt in the world than soap.
More hurt in the world than hope.

More need in the world than how.
More weed in the world than plough.

More walk in the world than shoe.
More talk in the world than do.

More bark in the world than bite.
More dark in the world than light.

More shame in the world than pride.
More lame in the world than ride.

More stick in the world than eat.
More trick in the world than treat.

More fake in the world than friend.
More break in the world than mend.

More fish in the world than net.
More wish in the world than get.

More lock in the world than key.
More them in the world than we.

JANUARY, 2006

'Do whatever your heart desires...'

Do whatever your heart desires,
  But do it soon, do it soon;
Gathering years will gutter the fires—
  Bright the sun but pale the moon.
    Do it soon, do it soon.

Chase whichever the dream you nursed,
  But do it well, do it well;
Swallow the best, spit out the worst—
  Tell the mockers: *'Rot in hell!'*
    Do it well, do it well.

Wed whomever will love you long,
  But do it now, do it now;
Smother your lover in light and song—
  All is dark beneath the plough.
    Do it now, do it *now!*

JULY, 2004

Dry Season

A sun-baked cedar leaf scrapes by my chair;
In dappled shade I stroke the parent's bole
And scoop its leather offspring to my care:
A cast out victim: symptom of the whole—
The dead dry days are passing in a rush;
The world is topsy-turvy. Seasons lie,
And what should be a desert now is lush,
While back in England arid snowdrops die.
The wisest of the wise debate a cause,
Man-made— or else some cycle of the sun;
Yet nature shuns indifferent applause
For causes; what is done has long been done.
    Come now, my friends, the change, perhaps, is real,
    But let us break no 'traitors' on the wheel!

MARCH, 2006

Many environmental fundamentalists (eco-Nazis, I call 'em) are quick to point the finger and swift with their doom-mongering advice. Let them read this, a précis in 'The Week' magazine August 31, 2007 from an original article in 'The Boston Globe':

"If there's anything climate-change crusaders are adamant about," writes Jeff Jocoby, "it is that the science of the matter is settled." But it's not. In fact, science's view of how the climate will be affected by green-house gas emissions "changes all the time," with some very reputable scientists questioning whether a man-made disaster is looming at all. NASA administrator Michael Griffin recently pointed out that the climate has been fluctuating for millennia, and that it's arrogant to assume we now possess "the optimal climate." Scientists recently admitted that their understanding of future sea-level rises is "limited," and dropped estimates from the catastrophic 3 feet trumpeted by Al Gore to 17 inches. This month, climate scientists had to admit that 1998 was not the hottest year on record after all— 1934 was. After an error was found in previous data, in fact, it turns out that five of the hottest years in the U.S. occurred <u>before</u> 1940, with only three in the last decade. Do these mistakes mean global warming is entirely a myth? No, but it does mean that "the science of climate change is still young and unsettled," with years of trial and error ahead of us.

I am not saying we should do nothing. But I argue strongly that the rantings and terror tactics of eco-Nazi crusaders is counter-productive, as well as suspect in its motive. Beware of Jeremiahs. The world is as full of them today as it has always been. Perhaps it makes them feel important to make the flesh of others creep and to boss us about. But let us remember this: they know little more than we— and many know a damn sight less.

Eight Deadly Sins

Pride, a wreck where hope once stood—
Envy, grief for a neighbour's good—
Cant and anger bring to **Wrath**
Defective love, the root of **Sloth**—

Weak-kneed **Avarice** covets all—
While **Gluttony** grooms **Lust** to crawl
Beside him, trembling, bathed in sweat—
Lord cleanse thy servant, but not yet!

FEBRUARY, 2006

These are the seven deadly (or capital) sins as distinguished by Pope Gregory in the 6th century, in order of severity, starting with **Pride**, 'the beginning of every sin'. To Gregory's seven I have added an eighth: Augustine's sin of **Prevarication** summed up in book 8 of his Confessions three centuries earlier: '[Lord,] give me chastity and continence, but not yet'. Which, I guess, is how most of us feel on that subject most of the time. As to 'Defective love, the root of sloth', this came from my reading of a translation of Aquinas in which he argues that all sins are derived, one way and another, from love, and that 'sloth is grief for Divine, spiritual love.' This sounds like baloney, until you read his powerful argument.

Empire: A Valediction

Unruly whelps of language and the sea,
    An isle of grocers, steeped in class and loss,
Who like to dip digestives in their tea—
    Whose Finest Hour is now their Albatross.

JANUARY, 2004

'I fear the wind...'

I fear the wind— I always did,
Its scudding tides of dread and doubt;
And as a child, wherever I hid,
The wind would always find me out.

I feared the crocodile sob of air,
The shriek of tortured trees outside;
'The Devil's abroad in coach and pair,'
My Nan would sniff, *'no use to hide.'*

But I fear the wind, it's eerie tongue,
The clatter of nameless things in flight—
For I have known, since I was young,
That I shall die on a stormy night.

FEBRUARY, 2005

'Fair is foul in heat...'

Fair is foul in heat.
Bone is sweet in meat.
Mirth abandons dread.
Cruel is kind in bed.
Loss is gain to heirs.
Love is proof to stares.
Lame is whole in mind.
Near is far, behind.
Fear deserts the bold,
Keys are locks when old.
Kill is cure to pride.
Mock is death to side.
A fist is just a hand—
Depending where you stand.

MARCH, 2006

Father, Dear

(for Leon Mannings)

To never show that you're afraid,
To learn that men may cry,
To plant a tree beneath whose shade
Another man shall lie;

To stop and ask the way when lost,
To sometimes not be sure,
To swallow hard and bear the cost,
Else, what are fathers for?

To do their homework, fix the shelf,
To love your birthday socks,
To keep your feelings to yourself
Concerning boys and frocks;

To walk them here, to drive them there,
To praise a new tattoo,
To whistle when they dye their hair
Bright platinum or blue;

To read their boyfriend out his rights,
To know he's not the first,
To stay awake most Friday nights
Imagining the worst.

To chivy luck, to soothe their fears,
To spit upon the odds —
If fathers did all this, my dears,
Then fathers would be gods!

AUGUST, 2003

Fear nothing!

Fear nothing! What is terror? Fears writ large,
    To clamp a claw across our cringing neck
When battleships called Courage shrink to barge
    And, turning turtle, drown us in the wreck.

To sail a Sea of Fear is no disgrace,
    Though some might say it is; fools yet to learn
The fates permit no compass in this race:
    The shipwreck of our hope lies just astern.

Fear nothing! Fear itself is fed by fear,
    And all fears pass. Did no one tell you so?
Come take, my friend, and we will peer
    Into this fear's abyss. To jump. To *know*.

FEBRUARY, 2005

In Defence of Hope

Though hope betrays us each in turn
    And is by time itself betrayed,
Though in its forge we roast and burn,
    Still cursing as the embers fade —

Amid the ash of ruined dreams
    We persevere, against all odds,
While any speck of hope yet gleams
    To stand against the whims of gods.

If hope is but a fuel to scorch
    What men think lost, with fate the spark,
At least it counterfeits a torch
    To hoist aloft and dupe the dark.

JULY, 2002

Homeless in My Heart

Like Ulysses, I sailed and flew,
    A weary metronome
In search of time, yet never knew
    The measured beat of home.

A wanderer— his flag unfurled
    Wherever he might fly,
A secret son who strode the world
    Has only now learned why…

My mind cries out to startled hands
    'Tear up the map, the chart:
This creature of a thousand lands
    Is homeless in his heart.'

MARCH, 2006

'The estuaries of hell...'

The estuaries of hell are wide;
    The barges (Satan's special pride)
Provide for those who wish to ride
    One way; for just as advertised
The ferries are all subsidised.

JANUARY, 2001

House Rules

We play in the House of Original Sin,
Where the name of the game is Blame,
Where Habit and Guilt take turns to spin
And credit is measured in Shame;
Where the wheel is rigged, the fix is in,
And the rules stay always the same:
You cannot break even; you cannot win;
And you cannot get out of the game.

JULY, 2003

In the three principal Laws of Thermodynamics, (there are four, but we needn't go into that), the First states that energy cannot be created, the Second that some energy is always wasted (no perpetual motion possible) and the Third that you can never reduce temperatures to absolute zero. As Bill Bryson notes in his *A Short History of Nearly Everything* (Doubleday 2003), these laws are sometimes expressed jocularly by physicists as follows: (1) you can't win, (2) you can't break even, and (3) you can't get out of the game. This struck me as a sound summation for the human condition, never mind thermodynamics!

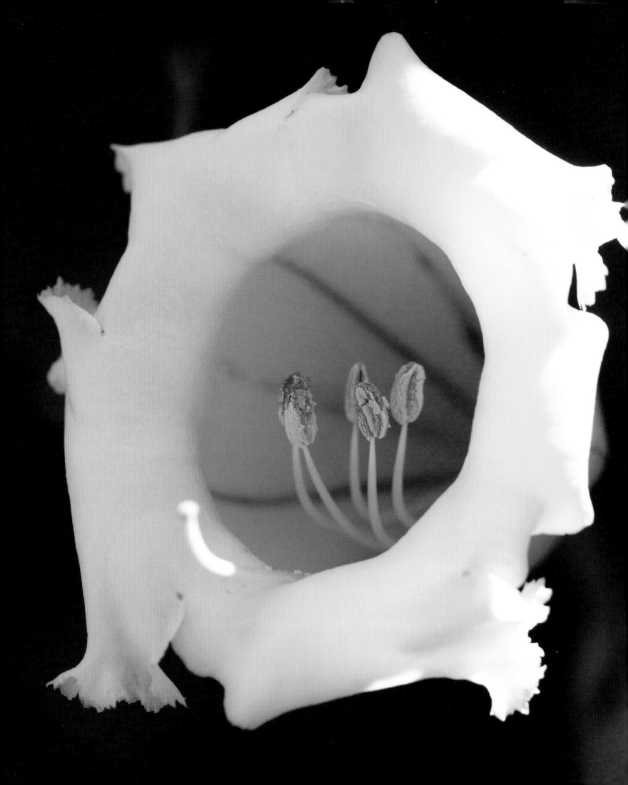

'I am listening, now...'

I am listening, now. The past is past,
I'm here. I'm sitting beside your bed.
Speak to me now. It's time at last
To make amends. The past is dead.

I am listening, now. I'm here, my dear.
Your spotted hands are soft as fur.
Speak to me, now. I've ears to hear,
They are not so deaf as once they were.

I am listening, now. I'm done with fuss;
Babble of treachery, love or pain,
Speak of yourself, of them, of us—
Speak of the ghosts that fill the rain.

I am listening, now. I left it late,
Later than ever we thought or knew.
Speak to me. Please. Unbar the gate.
Turn back, my dear. I'm here for you.

JANUARY, 2005

'...but the rain is full of ghosts tonight...'
— Edna St. Vincent Millay

Armoured in Innocence

(March 17, 1968)

Marching together to Grosvenor Square,
The tribes in their finery, off to the fair,
What were we marching for, why were we there?
Angels and anarchists, hunter and prey,
Chanting our nursery-rhymes on the way:
'Hey, Hey! LBJ!
How many kids did you bomb today!'

Where were we marching to?
What was it for?
Which was the enemy?
Where was the war?

Armoured in innocence, Tolkein and weed,
Crawling on waterbeds, rapping on speed,
Passionate, indolent, sure of our creed,
Reading Marcusé and missing the rent,
Crashing with strangers from Goa to Ghent,
'Hey, Hey! LBJ!
How many dreams did you crush today!'

Who were we shouting at?
What did we know?
Whose were the dreams we dreamed?
Where did they go?

Ferried and buried in mud on the Wight,
Building a city of love overnight,
Dervishes whirling and tripping the light,
Writhing and raving, splattered in paint,
Choking and toking and ready to faint,
'Hey, Hey! LBJ!
How many tabs did you drop today!'

Who were we dancing with?
How many hours?
Where are the songs we sung?
Whose are these flowers?

AUGUST, 2003

'I just stepped out...'

Where am I? — Oh, I just stepped out,
No need to make a fuss, or shout,
No need to comb the nearest wood
Or roam about the neighbourhood.

Call off the dog— she'll find no scent,
Please don't worry where I went,
And do not climb the garden tree,
My dear, you'll catch no glimpse of me.

The attic steps will pinch your thumb,
The cellar will be dark and dumb,
Yet should you search your heart with care,
Though I am gone, you'll find me there.

JUNE, 2007

'I sleep alone...'

I sleep alone... to loosen tongue-tied joints,
    (My body lies too still for company),
Its rag doll limbs adrift like compass points.
    I sleep alone... because I need to be.

I sleep alone... because I sometimes fart,
    Because I lie awake in shiftless drift,
My mind astride the hoof-beats of my heart,
    I sleep alone... to hide a grievous gift.

I sleep alone... to snore, and cough, and read,
    To vivisect old demons in the dark.
My savage dreams accustomed to their need,
    I sleep alone... lest hidden fuses spark.

I sleep alone... to shield myself from shame,
    To stifle panic's press in privacy,
Each sweated cloth a winding sheet of flame,
    I sleep alone... so none shall ever see.

I sleep alone... though once, in light-foot youth,
    Our beds were rendezvous for idle lust,
And if I miss your silk-soft flesh — in truth,
    I sleep alone, my dear, because I must.

JANUARY, 2004

In Reflection

No matter that my duty is to love her—
    Love is a daughter's place:
I shall not let myself become my mother,
    Nor wear her face.

No matter if my mirror shares her features,
    Self is a state of mind,
Nor if my hand betrays another creature's:
    All glass is blind.

No matter that my smile is like another—
    Flesh of her flesh and bone:
I shall not let myself become my mother:
    My life's my own.

JANUARY, 2004

'All women become like their mothers.
That is their tragedy. No man does. That's his.'
— Oscar Wilde, 'The Importance of Being Earnest'

'Kohl'

Our big, black, faithful dog has died,
I found him, lying on his side
Splayed on the rug, beside the bed:
Our big, black, faithful dog is dead.

Never a whimper, never a whine,
His coat like midnight, eyes a-shine,
A lion's heart, a fool to bribe,
The gentleman of all his tribe.

My lover's friend, and my friend, too,
Has gone— as we bid Kohl adieu
And many a foolish tear is shed:
Our big, black, faithful dog is dead.

AUGUST, 2006

Laughing Buddha

Laughing Buddha in the sand,
Spade and bucket in your hand,
Newly-minted, wonder-eyed,
Architect of time and tide;

Mischief written on your brow,
Master of the here-and-now,
Free of past and future's taint,
Life the canvas, joy the paint;

Sorcerer of sea and sky,
Innocent of where or why,
Perfect in your symmetry —
Wanting nothing but to *be*.

Offspring of a dream deferred,
Fill your bucket; speak no word!
Hoard your secrets; stop your ears!
Alphabets spell only tears.

You who sit in Eden's shade,
Teasing angels with your spade,
Empty-headed, eyes of blue —
We were once as wise as you.

Infant Buddha, sifting sand,
All creation in your hand,
Where does infant wisdom fly?
Heaven only knows — not I.

JANUARY, 2003

I was on Pasture Beach rereading Peter Matthiessen's limpid sojourn into Buddhism and Nepal, *The Snow Leopard*, and had reached a chapter of his musings concerning holy men who live only in the here and now *(or Now!* as he irritatingly puts it) having attained sufficient wisdom to see through the camouflage of past and future — when it occurred to me that such a creature was right in front of me. A toddler furiously digging on the beach, oblivious to his surroundings, utterly content with his lot and not a thought in his head but to dig, dig, dig! Even the (apparent) uselessness of his self-appointed task fitted Matthiessen's glorious description of epiphany-in-action. I scratched the first four lines of 'Laughing Buddha' in the sand with a stick — having neglected to bring a pencil with me. By next morning, only 'Architect of time and tide' had survived the waves' incursions.

Where Does the Soul Live?

Where does the soul live? Not in here,
    Not in this flurry of fingers and thumbs
    Plundering thunder from other men's drums:
Though books have spines — not here.

Where is it hiding? Not in here,
    Not in the teeth of a charlatan's kiss
    Wedged at the brink of its own abyss:
Though tongues may err — not here.

Where does the soul sit? Not in here,
    Not in this covert of bramble and briar
    That hems the sphere of its own desire:
Though hairs grow grey — not here.

Where is it lurking? Not in here,
    Not in this moat where the white cells wait
    For foreign assassins behind the gate:
Though veins run deep — not here.

Where does the soul sleep? Not in here,
    Not in these Alice-in-Wonderland sighs
    Where the Jabberwock dries his vorpal eyes:
Though mirrors lie — not here.

Where is it feeding? Not in here.
    Not in the silt of a born-again sieve
    Filtering faults we forgot to forgive:
Though memory fades — not here.

Where does the soul live? Is it *here*?
    Here in this no-man's trench, consigned
    To bind each 'I' to an orphaned mind?
Is this where the soul lives — here?

JANUARY, 2003

Love is a Loaded Taser

Love is a loaded taser
　　Pointed at my heart;
A finger falters... squeezes... fires
A jolt of pain and joy on wires,
To spear me with its razor
　　Sharpened dart.
Love knows nothing of our desires,
Nor cares which corpses crowd its shrine:
Whose finger loosed this bolt of
　　Love but mine?

DECEMBER, 2005

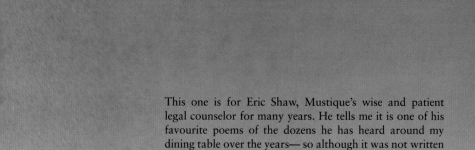

This one is for Eric Shaw, Mustique's wise and patient legal counselor for many years. He tells me it is one of his favourite poems of the dozens he has heard around my dining table over the years— so although it was not written on Mustique (I composed it while flying over Greenland on the way to New York City) I have included it here.

taser: noun: US trademark: a weapon firing barbs attached by wires to batteries, causing temporary paralysis.
Origin: 1970's from *Tom Swift's electric rifle* on the pattern of *laser*.
— New Oxford Dictionary of English
(Oxford University Press 1998)

Memory

(for Robert Woof)

Soon enough, the idling scythe
Gathers us to his embraces;
Yet in one place - still - that tithe
Neither triumphs, nor effaces:
Bright in memory, you lie,
And shall gleam there, till I die.

Memory, sweet memory;
Death, I make a mock of thee!

Soon enough, come weal and woe;
Even those whose hearts were golden
Bend beneath the tyrant's blow;
Now, to none, are you beholden:
In our memories, you lie:
We shall share them, by and by.

Bound by memory are we;
Death, we make a mock of thee!

Soon enough, our stories end,
Some in glory, some sore-smitten;
No fine words can make amend,
Yet, on this last page is written:
'Forged in memory, you lie,
And shall blaze there, till we die.'

Memory, sweet memory;
Death, we make a mock of thee!

FEBRUARY, 2006

I only met Robert towards the end of his life. But I was fortunate to get to know him well enough to recognise a true scholar, an inspiring teacher and a wonderful man. His work as Director of the Wordsworth Trust in Grasmere stands as a towering epitaph to his talents and exuberant energies. In addition to single-handedly creating a collection of international importance at Grasmere, now the Centre for British Romanticism, he inaugurated an inspirational series of poetry readings and artist-in-residence programmes there. All this was achieved while he and his wife, Pamela, continued their own researches and writing in addition to publishing some of the most beautifully produced catalogues for exhibitions imaginable. Countless young poets, artists, scholars, students, lovers of the Romantic Poets and an entire community - indeed the whole of his country - stand deeply in his debt. As Wordsworth himself wrote, following the death of his brother John, "Not without hope we suffer and we mourn." Not without hope, no. But to lose a man like Robert Woof is hard because of the yawning vacuum left in the wake of so formidable and loveable a genius. A very great man.

Dear Mr. & Mrs. Bananaquit

Dear Mr. & Mrs. Bananaquit,
I've a bone to pick with you both, I fear;
Could I please suggest you <u>do not nest</u>
Inside my chandelier this year!

There's plenty of space to pile your sticks
In the lemon bush or the cedar tree,
But it's frightfully queer in a chandelier,
And besides, it blocks the light, you see?

And on top of all that the wiring's bad,
And its awfully, awfully hot inside,
As a mom and dad, it must be sad
To find that most of your eggs have fried...

So, Mr. and Mrs. Bananaquit,
I beg you to stop and to listen to me:
Please keep well clear of my chandelier!
   Yours very sincerely,
    Mr. D.

APRIL, 2001

My Garden By The Sea

Oh, would you like to come with me,
Down to my garden by the sea,
Far, far away in Caribbee?

Where the sun beats down from a lazy sky
And hammerhead clouds go sailing by;
Where the tor...tois...es...plod...oh...so...slow,
And the humming birds flash to and fro
By the lily ponds and the waterfalls,
Where geckos bask on sun-baked walls
    Under the giant shak-shak tree —
    Here in my garden, by the sea.

Where the fireflies wink like fairy lights
Beneath tall palms on velvet nights,
And the scent of the frangipani flowers
As tree-frogs whistle in the wee-wee hours,
And the hiss of the surf in a starlit glow
While sailboats rock in the bay below,
    Rocking, rocking, silently —
    Beneath my garden, by the sea.

Let's run away, just you and me,
Down to my garden by the sea,
Far, far away in Caribbee!

JANUARY, 2001

Life Support

Upon a bed of ice and fire,
    I waited, swathed in tube and wire,
        My lungs a searing funeral pyre:
            They asked me my religion — I was dying.
Grown weary in the fever's grip
    I watched an intravenous drip
        Pump ballast, then abandoned ship;
            'He's sinking!' cried a nurse. I thought: *I'm flying!*

Much later, while I convalesced
    I learned what I'd already guessed,
        When on his rounds, a quack confessed:
            'We nearly lost you, son. You just weren't trying.
I've seen it once or twice before...
    You wandered through an open door
        But can't remember what you saw?'
        'You're right,' I said. And found that I was crying.

JULY, 2001

With sincere thanks to the doctors, nurses
and diagnosticians of Danbury Hospital,
Connecticut, who (not to put too fine a point
on it) saved my life in September 1988.

'All sunsets are illusions to the eye...'

All sunsets are illusions to the eye;
No sun has ever set from mortal sight —
Our puny ball of mud spins in the sky
To stare upon the void men call the night.

All gods are but the churn of plow to seeds,
The chaff of priests mere superstitious cant.
Their words are perilous, judge by their deeds!
Their prophets profitless, mere beards and rant.

When imams pray in interstellar space
Five times a day — pray, which way must they face?
When bishops rage at inter-species love,
Shall demons mock below — or screech above?

All sunsets are illusions to the eye;
And we ourselves are gods— and all gods die.

DECEMBER, 2002

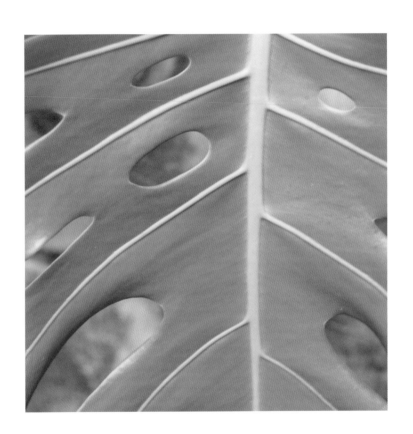

'Though misery loves company...'

Though misery loves company
    Wherever it is found,
Think carefully before you toss
    Your agony around.

The hurt will pass, and presently
    The only blot in sight,
Will be the sot you foolishly
    Confessed to, one dark night.

MARCH, 2006

Of Debts and Mothers

The wiser man forgets what he forgives,
Discarding debts as lesser mortal's toys,
No man grows old while yet his mother lives:
To mothers, mighty kings are careless boys.

DECEMBER, 2003

'Brother, can you paradigm?'

Where would poets be
If we slew the simile —
Redundant as a dolphin on a bike!
Let the semi-literati
Play the poopers at the party:
I never metaphor I didn't like.

AUGUST, 2003

William Saffire's 'On Language' column in *The New York Times* is a glorious American institution. With its Lexicographic Irregulars (a nod to Sherlock Holmes's gang of street urchins), the Squad Squad (redundancy spotters) and assorted Phrasedicks, Nitpickers' League and Gotcha! Gang members, Saffire has created an alternative universe supremely suited for those of us curious about (or intoxicated with) language. Both the title and the last line of the doggerel above came from a collection of his columns in book form: 'In Love With Norma Loquendi', (Random House 1994). Fairness compels me to point out that the last line was taken from a letter addressed to Mr. Saffire by one Herman Gross from Great Neck, New York.

'This is the Server...'

I

This is the Server, waiting on station,
Silicone god of an e-mail nation,

Bearing you news of a baby boy,
Bringing you misery, bringing you joy —

Telling you auntie has taken to pottery,
Gloating your ex has won the lottery,

Jottings ethereal, letters venereal,
Packets attaching the oddest material,

Bleating that Katie has married a fool,
Reminding you "Man' United rule!"

Enclosing a last demand from creditors,
Filing a blast to newspaper editors,

Begging the pardon of furious lovers,
Shopping for pillows and sofa covers,

Juggling schedules, checking arrivals,
Flattering bosses, flattening rivals,

Laden with rumours and odious jokes
Featuring zebras and artichokes...

II

Servant of presidents, servant of hacks,
Blinking and winking in towering stacks,

Serving up poetry, panic and porn,
Dishing the dirt from dusk til dawn,

Guarding the gospels of new messiahs,
Tracking the passage of forest fires,

Plotting an expedition to Everest,
Funding your local neighbourhood terrorist,

Bidding for first editions of Keats,
Cribbing your homework, booking your seats,

Checking if Daddy has taken his medicine,
Clinching the date of birth for Edison,

Gathering evidence, paying your taxes,
Ordering pizza and beer from Max's,

Auctioning Fords and a red Mercedes,
(All of them owned by little old ladies),

Shooting the breeze and playing at *Doom*,
A long-legged fly in a steel-racked room...

➤

III

The Server has crashed!
The Server is down!
The screens have dimmed in city and town,
The emperor stripped of his digital gown,
The babbling web is lame and halt,
Its pillars of Silicone ground to salt —
Default! Default!
Default! Default!

The Server is up!
The Server is back!
The techies have purged a hacker attack,
The natter and chatter is back on track,
The terminal drives have held their nerve,
The Server survives — and as you observe —
I serve! I serve!
I serve! I serve!

APRIL, 2003

(With fond acknowledgement
to W.H. Auden's great poem
'Night Train' which served as
the inspiration for this poem.)

Breakfast on Mustique

Ghost koi, their sunflower-yellow button eyes
Unstitched, weave shadows in the morning sun
And suck on moss-backed stones. The tree ants run
Patrols, their only thought to tyrannise
Some hapless aphid. Scab-red dragon-flies
Patrol just out of reach, jaws poised to stun
Their careless prey and drain them, one by one.
Night lilies fold away amidst the cries
Of Bequia-sweets at table, sword-sharp beaks
Extended — each scrap of food defended
From its neighbour. A tortoise heaves and wins
First prize: hibiscus flowers! Our kitten sneaks
Some bacon. The hungry night has ended;
Another day in Paradise begins.

JANUARY, 2002

Olives from Gethsemane

Friend, if you have POWER thrust
Upon your lap, to hold in trust,
Place it under lock and key,
Keep yourself most solitary.

Guard it well by day and night,
Suffer none to share your plight,
You, who never knew a FOE,
Now must learn what PRINCES know:

All men born, both young and old,
Covet that one FRUIT you hold,
Scheming of its FLESH and CORE,
Dreaming they may taste it raw.

'Ware the worm within its HEART!
Peel and wrap each rotten part,
Gift it to your ENEMY —
Olives from GETHSEMANE.

JULY, 2002

On some days...

On some days, everything is wrong. Why is this?
    The milk is off. Your words dry up. Thoughts fail.
And though you know the fault is yours, you miss
    The days when neither thought, nor bread, was stale.

And yet, on other days, your touch is sure.
    Friends laugh. Cats purr. A fumbler could not miss.
Bone china will not shatter on the floor.
    On some days, everything goes right. Why is this?

FEBRUARY, 2006

'Pass Me De Banana Wine...'

Dem politicians on de take,
    An' what dey take be mine,
De pack o' dem be sham an' fake,
Dey vex me wid de belly-ache
    — Pass me de banana wine.

Me loss' de crop, no rum, no bread,
    De fruit die on de vine,
De 'elicopter spray dem dead
To keep us we from bein' fed
    — Pass me de banana wine.

De wife she gone, she run away,
    Me read de note she sign.
She say me make too lickle pay,
Play too much domino all day
    — Pass me de banana wine.

Dey say dey lock me in de jail
    Where sun don' never shine,
Me got nobody go me bail,
De food be bad, de water stale
    — Pass me de banana wine.

Me ax de warden for a drink,
    Dey give me turpentine,
Nobody love me now, I t'ink,
I standin' on the very brink
    — Pass me de banana wine.

AUGUST, 2002

The people of St. Vincent & the Grenadines do not spell 'the' as 'de', nor do they spell 'they' as 'dey' nor 'them' as 'dem' nor 'ask' as 'ax'. But that is how most Vincentians pronounce them and I have spelt them as such as an *aide-mémoire* for reading aloud. Substitution of 'me' for 'I' is widespread in the Caribbean as is the inversion of words in certain phrases. The word 'vex' is common, although virtually extinct in British 'received' English. Politicians are widely held to be corrupt, so that even honest reformers are often tarred with their predecessors' brush. The US helicopters which used to come to spray the mountain marijuana fields caused great damage to fruit crops and were universally detested as an invasion of national sovereignty. 'Banana wine' is slang for a pesticide used by banana farmers to clear away weeds and harmful insects from their crop. It is also drunk as a cheap, hideously painful form of suicide. My thanks to Yolande, Webb, Jennifer and Baba at Mandalay House for the idea for this ballad — and for correcting my vernacular usage.

Perfect Day

Today was one of the best days of my life.
Nothing of any importance occurred—
I cut my finger on a paperknife
And marvelled at a busy hummingbird
Plucking out wet moss by a waterfall;
Broke bread with friends and shared a glass of wine;
Wrote this poem; swam; made love. That's all.
Why should it be some days erect a shrine…
A cairn, a white stone day, in memory?
Is it, as Buddhists claim, a lack of need,
Or want? Or simple serendipity,
The perfect flowering of one small seed?
    The wise will say our frames are none too pure:
    How many perfect days could we endure?

AUGUST, 2007

Poetry is...

Poetry is not a trade,
Nor even a profession—
Poetry is what is made
By pagans at confession.

Verse is an emolument
In lieu of pay or ration,
The crafting of an argument
Need distills from passion.

Verse is love, ennui or rage
As idle fates disown us:
Poetry will pay no wage—
It is itself its bonus.

APRIL, 2006

Aye, it is. And so much more. In this little book for my friends and neighbours on Mustique, I will make a confession that I shall not repeat beneath this poem should it be reprinted elsewhere. It is this: poetry saved my life when I had nearly thrown it away. To be strictly truthful, it saved me when I did not care if I threw it away or not. I do not claim to have written even one good poem; but that is not the point. The act of attempting to do so, and of reading and analysing so many great poets along the way, helped heal me. It continues to do so. Should you ever find yourself in despair or deeply troubled, try poetry.

Putting Licky Down

What is it, then, you say to them
    When medics shake their head;
When heaving lungs are thick with phlegm,
    Your old bitch marked for dead?

What salve is there to comfort eyes
    That trust beyond their pain —
What right have I, when all hope dies,
    To whimper, or complain?

Her days were mischief, sleep and play,
    Her tongue a children's shrine,
She stole some hearts along the way —
    And one of them was mine.

What's left to do but stroke her flanks
    And kiss her half-pricked ear?
What bridge have I to make my thanks?
    Good night. God speed, my dear.

JULY, 2003

Licky was an orange ball of fur who lived a long life and produced many puppies. I inherited her when I bought my house on Mustique from David Bowie. Beloved by every child who ever met her, she sat at my feet in my study for more evenings than I can count. Even now I look down occasionally when writing, expecting her familiar white muzzle to be staring up at me.

Safe in Port

My floating fort lies safe in port,
And not a drop is spilt,
A creeping tide buoys up my pride:
Was that why ships were built?

While other craft sail port and aft
My thoughts of voyages fade,
Salt tears and guilt make fearsome silt:
Was that why hearts were made?

JULY, 2006

Seven Tides

The first and second tides bleat soft, like sheep;
So soft are they, their waters barely creep
Past infant castles patted in a heap.
The third grows breasts and bristles on the neap;
Upon the fourth our fortunes toss and leap;
The wicked fifth claims what we thought to reap.
The sixth arrives by stealth, while greybeards sleep;
The seventh comes: short terrors — and the deep.

MARCH, 2006

Am I the Only One?

Am I the only one so blessed,
  The one your green-eyed goddess spurns—
Who shrugs when love deserts the nest
  And shrugs again when she returns;

Who wryly welcomes flesh or word
  From moths who fan some other flame;
Who hears you out, but thinks absurd
  These salves for needless scabs of shame?

For is not 'love' a child of need,
  No matter how the sonnets run?
Why bare a wound where guilt will breed?
  And am I, then— the only one?

AUGUST, 2007

Or, as the mystery writer Dorothy L. Sayers once put it:

> As I grow older and older
> And totter toward the tomb
> I find that I care less and less
> Who goes to bed with whom.

Me too, Dorothy; me too. Except that is how I have felt all my life!

Song for a Child, Newly Born

(for Patsy Fisher)

May your thoughts be with the living,
    May your hand and eye be swift,
May your thanks be with the giving
    And never with the gift.

May your kindness be unfailing,
    May your ship pass by each shoal,
May the helmsman of each sailing
    Be the captain of your soul.

May you pass through all life's dangers,
    May your lovers all be true,
May you learn that this world's strangers
    Were friends you never knew.

May your laughter ring like fountains,
    May your heart be wild and free,
May you walk among the mountains
    But live beside the sea.

DECEMBER, 2004

Patsy Fisher passed away in November 2006. She is survived by her husband Bud, her daughter, Nicole and her son, Adam. Universally beloved on Mustique — indeed, universally loved wherever she went — Patsy was one of those rare human beings it was impossible not to admire. Born in Brazil, she lived for many years in Canada and 'retired' with Bud to Mustique. The word 'retired' needs inverted commas because Patsy would have laughed at such a description: as a talented artist whose watercolours grace innumerable homes around the world and as an inveterate traveller, reader and teacher, Patsy never stopped trying to help those around her. Quite simply, she radiated good will, combining laughter without malice, kindness without sentimentality and warm-hearted help to all who sought her out, as so many did. I have never met a better person and suspect I never shall. Her husband, Bud, summed up her life beautifully at a memorial service in our Bamboo Church: "In all the years of our marriage, I never once came home to a bad mood or an angry word." The poem was one I wrote in 2004 and was a favourite of Patsy's. Without knowing it, perhaps, I had composed 'Song for a Child, Newly Born' with Patsy Fisher as its model and inspiration.

Song of the Serpents

Men are older than they know,
    But not so old as Guilt,
Guilt was on the Knowledge Tree
    Before the world was built.

Men are wiser than they think,
    But not so wise as We,
Wise men lack the span of years
    To see as serpents see.

Men are prouder than is wise,
    But not so proud as Dust,
Dust bows not to men or gods
    To mantle what it must.

Men are weaker than they wish,
    Yet not so weak as Death,
Death must nurse its midwife, Life,
    To rob her brother, Breath.

Serpents fuse the skein of Life,
    Their venom at its throat;
Love is stronger than men know,
    Yet yields no antidote.

JULY, 2002

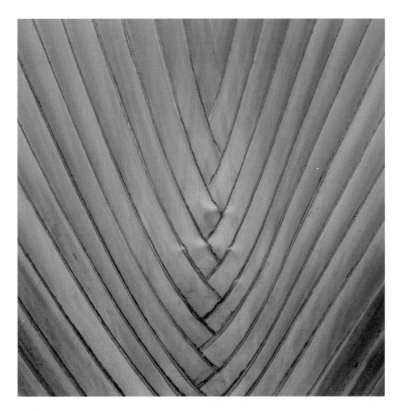

What a delicious irony that the shape of the DNA molecule, which defines the physical characteristics of all life, should so resemble a pair of serpents. Or perhaps not. The medical profession has used a similar device for centuries.

Subha's Picture

To Subha Chinnayan, the Girl who Drew the Tsunami

Others shall tell, with more power than I,
Of the Day of the Wave, of the Judas sky,
Of the sun that cozened the bay and the land,
Of the scouring shudder of racing sand,
Of curious looks, of a puzzled pause,
Of the far-off rumble of earth's applause,
Of the sea sucked up like milk from a dish,
Of a miracle harvest of flopping fish,
Of glistening pools as the sea withdrew,
Of the growing panic of those who knew,
Of silence— pierced by the cry of a wife,
Of a boy beginning the race of his life,
Of toddlers digging with bucket and spade
With minutes to live; of the roar it made,
The roar of rabid, insentient beast,
Raving and ravenous, eager to feast...

Of Nature's assassin, blotting the sky,
Others must tell, with more power than I.

But...

Of Subha's drawing, her guileless art,
Of a picture that tears at the mind and heart,
Of an infant scrawl of pain and rage,
Of her name and date at the top of the page,
Of heads without faces, of limbs in an 'X',
Of shattered debris, of fragment and wrecks,
Of huts and houses upon their side,
Of carnage in crayon, of boats that died,
Of trees uprooted, of jumbled woes,
Of friends and neighbours laid out in rows,
Of a day when the world was put to flight,
Of Subha— to Chitra's daughter, I write:

Though your too-wise eyes will never read this,
A hug for you Subha, a hug and a kiss,
May the gods of memory grant you peace,
May the power of youth bring sweet release,
May your children be many, happy and strong,
And the Day of the Wave a tale in a song.

JANUARY, 2005

Subha Chinnayan was a twelve year old girl from the village of Keechangkuppam on the Tamil Nadu coast of south India. The village was wiped out by the Boxing Day, 2004 tsunami. She and her mother, Chitra, her brother and sister all survived. More than 700 others in the vicinity did not. She drew her picture of the wreckage and bodies littering her village while in a relief camp eight days after 'the day of the wave'. It was published on the front page of The Daily Telegraph in the UK, helping to raise millions of pounds for tsunami survivors. Her photograph appeared a week later in the same paper, where she was quoted as saying that however many tsunamis come "we will rebuild our house again. I am not frightened of the sea. My mother has told me not to be frightened." Subha's photograph depicts a young girl in pigtails and a brightly patterned blouse. The article says she is in Year Eight of her school — but her eyes, staring straight into the camera, are a million years old; they are eyes of our forbears from uncounted millennia crying out in defiance at the gods of chaos: "Do what you will. We shall survive!"

The Elephant in the Room

The elephant in the room that isn't there —
He's hard to walk around. He's big and grey.
My Mummy says it's not polite to stare.

He never moves. He can't fit in a chair,
Just standing there. He's always in the way,
The elephant in the room that isn't there.

Sometimes, at night, I send a little prayer
For God to shoo him out so I can play.
My Mummy says it's not polite to stare

And if I do, she ruffles up my hair
And asks me what I learned in school today.
The elephant in the room that isn't there

Has squashed us all apart. It isn't fair,
But if I ask about him what they say
Is: 'Mummy says it's not polite to stare.'

The grown-ups are pretending not to care —
We never ask how long he wants to stay.
Dear elephant in the room who isn't there,
My Mummy says it's not polite to stare.

JANUARY, 2004

The Endless War

Of good and evil's high decrees,
    The writ of earthly powers,
All men are but its refugees —
    This war was never ours.

And whether God or Satan fell
    I neither know nor care,
Nor know if Satan reigns in hell
    Or cast his master there.

Creators come, their prophets fall,
    We use their temple stone
To build a farm, to mend a wall,
    While preachers up and drone.

What kind of God requires praise
    To supplement His powers?
And what to us which slayer slays?
    This war was never ours.

AUGUST, 2003

Island Storm at Night

Shadows on the moonlit sea
Flit across the bay,
Storm clouds blot a star-filled sky,
Ominous and grey.

Ghostly frangipani flowers
Flicker in the light,
Tree frogs whistle up the wind —
There'll be rain tonight.

Lizards on the sun deck rail
Raise Jurassic heads,
Two manicou blink possum eyes
Perched upon the leads.

'Here it...' Plop! A warning drop,
Fat and wet and warm,
Splashes on my upturned face—
Herald of the storm;

'... comes!' Distant rolls of thunder
Drown my feeble cry,
Island rain to spear the land,
Javelins of sky

Come crashing on the drowsy dark,
Lightning sparks the rods,
While all around— in ecstasy,
Tree frogs praise their gods.

MARCH, 2006

It is difficult to explain to anyone who has not seen and heard it the power of a big tropical storm; it is unlike anything one experiences in most parts of Europe or America. The tree frogs, too, though tiny little creatures barely the size of a fingernail, become so excited when it rains that their whistling drowns out human speech. 'Manicou' is the island name for a South American marsupial scavenger. One look at them is enough to bring home how old their species is compared to the few million years of human existence— the size of a small cat, able to climb any wall, sharp white teeth and dextrous claws, mad pink eyes, a naked, prehesile tail and tufts of gingery fur which their young use to hitch a ride on their mother's back after they exit the pouch. Manicou make crocodiles look positively modern!

'The hand is ever sadder than the heart...'

The hand is ever sadder than the heart,
More used to worldly ways, perhaps; more strong,
Its fingers poised to prise each slight apart,
Grown intimate with what is right and wrong.

The eye is often wiser than the mind,
As craftsmen trust a glance and spurn to think.
As like seeks like, all beauty seeks its kind,
Though knowledge gnaws a nail and dare not blink.

The poet's child was father to the man:
Though men protest — the horse will hate the cart,
Though mothers slack the bit as best they can,
The hand grows ever sadder than the heart.

FEBRUARY, 2005

166

Visions of Unutterable Boredom
(A British Celt questions an Irish Missionary Concerning 'Heaven')

Are there no storms that sweep this paradise?
No gusting rain to drench a blessed one's wing?
No bitter cold— no brambles rimed with ice?
From where, then, do your thrushes herald spring?

MARCH, 2005

The Water Lily

Random order is the glory of the world,
Its wilding patterns hid from human ken,
A colander of carbon atoms hurled
Across one mutant ball — and hurled again.

Geometry and pattern form our tools;
Voodoo metaphysics shield our bliss.
Philosophers may scold— but nature rules,
Few dare to stare too long at the abyss.

The riddle of a gene pool is the dearth
Of lifeguards on patrol. Old Darwin's debt
To barnacles or Haldane's beetled earth
Explain the inexplicable — and yet . . .

A dappled fawn, the shapes of wood or stone,
A cresting wave, the dew in petals curled;
This water lily floating quite alone:
Blind chaos is the glory of the world.

'Chaos is perhaps at the bottom of everything..." wrote George Santayana in *The Life of Reason*. He didn't <u>want</u> to believe it; much of his life was spent in logical and painstaking refutation of the assertion — but he was too honest and admirable a philosopher to strike out the phrase once he had considered it and committed it to paper. No known 'lifeguards' exist within the ordering of the DNA gene pool, as our children and our children's children will shortly discover. As for Darwin's barnacles and Haldane's beetles, they are the harbingers of what is to come, if we wish it.

Old Year's Night, Mustique

Moonlight waltzes in the clouds
    To stir the silver sea,
The palms are waving in the wind:
    'Goodbye, goodbye, '03'

The wind has blown a billion years,
    With billions yet to be,
It nothing cares for 'auld lang syne':
    'Goodbye, goodbye, '03'

My cat has praised my lap and leapt
    To claw the cedar tree,
Her tail whips out a question mark:
    'Goodbye, goodbye, '03'

The year is dead, the wench has fled,
    What use this cup to me?
She never cared for 'auld lang syne':
    'Goodbye, goodbye, '03'

JANUARY, 2004

Thoth's Gift

The god Ammon remonstrates
with Thoth concerning the latter's
gift of the written word to Men.

I see they scratch on stone and bark
To tally days and years,
While slyer scribes now make their mark
To tabulate their fears.

A princely gift— and kindly meant—
Yet we may rue the day
You shewed them… this… impediment…
And led such minds astray.

The songs of old, of blood and wrath,
Of war and love now lie
Cold captive — I foretell you, Thoth,
This gift shall see gods die.

These 'alphabets' but grant them leave
In learning— to forget;
Nor shall their children's children grieve
For Ammon, Thoth or Set.

AUGUST, 2004

A story told by Socrates in Plato's Phaedrus. Ammon (the Greek form of Amen-ra) was the King of Egyptian gods. Thoth was the lunar god, master of the annals, law and, not surprisingly perhaps, of hieroglyphs. Set (or Seth) was a god considered the incarnation of evil, having murdered his brother, Osiris. And, indeed, Ammon was right. The collective memory of mankind encapsulated by writing, led, after many centuries, to the Enlightenment. Which, though forgotten by many today, still shines like a beacon in Western philosophy, beckoning mankind to renounce the cruelty, hatreds and endless wars which have been the one unremitting inheritance of organised religion. Thank you, Thoth. Thank you. (Although I know you never existed!)

No single, secret heart...

No single, secret heart has man,
    Our lives are like a city built
In labyrinth— whose chambers span
    The arches of our joy and guilt.

Our churches to cathedrals swell,
    We feast our friends in marbled halls,
Play hermit in some Spartan cell,
    Or emperor with gilded walls.

And knowing time must loosen them,
    Still, brick by brick and room by room
We raise our own Jerusalem —
    To find we have but raised a tomb.

APRIL, 2002

Three-Legged Monsters on Macaroni Beach

Kick off your shoes and take my hand,
    We'll race three-legged upon the sand,
And I'll pretend that I am you —
    A monster out of Monster Land.

The sea and sky have eyes of blue,
    The waves are whispering 'who is who?'
The palms cry out 'what could it be?'
    The gulls reply 'we wish we knew!'

And though you know that you're not me,
    Most eyes see what they want to see.
We'll plant our three-legged footprints here,
    And leave a monstrous mystery!

For mysteries are rare, I fear,
    And secrets are for sharing, dear.
When you are grown, shed never a tear
    For three-legged monsters, never a tear.

DECEMBER, 2002

Time is the Cruel River

Time is the cruel river,
    The never ending stream,
The taker and the giver,
    A nightmare and a dream.

Its waters never waver,
    No bargain can be struck;
Its cruelty or favour
    Depend alone on luck.

Its current unencumbered
    By pity or by pride,
Its denizens outnumbered
    Within a deadly tide.

Our lives hang by a sliver
    From the hour we are born:
Time is the cruel river,
    And we are but its spawn.

JANUARY, 2006

To the Power of Three

Three sounds there have been since the world began
Before there were ears to hear:
The drumming of rain and the wind's great roar,
The hiss of a wave on a shingled shore,
For ever and ever...
    a wave on the shore,
Before there were ears to hear.

Three sights there have been since the world began,
Before there were curious eyes:
The sun and the moon and the star-strewn night
To cover the world with a pitiless light,
For ever and ever...
    that pitiless light,
Before there were curious eyes.

Three things there have been since the world began,
And perhaps shall ever be so:
The shuddering land caught fast in a vice,
The rivers of fire, the ravening ice,
For ever and ever...
    the fire and the ice,
And I think, shall ever be so.

APRIL, 2003

Turtle Shell Lamps

You do not like them? Neither do I,
But I will not smash or grind them up
In a great pretence. All things must die —
Some for a cause and some for a cup
Of turtle soup — but where's the sense
In judging such things by modern ways?
Regret, perhaps, for the ignorance
Of those long dead; for a passing phase
For ivory, or a sealskin hat,
For shark's-fin soup, or the eggs of birds
We scavenged to death. But as for that,
The world can never be changed by words,
Nor by the shadows of stones long thrown:
You leave my turtle shell lamps alone!

FEBRUARY, 2007

Well, there they hang on the wall, as they hung on another's wall for many and many a year. Just as the great bone hunter, poet and science writer, Loren Eiseley, used to keep the smashed skull of a biped older than sin — far older, sin not having been invented — on his desk, so my old turtle shell lamps are mute testimony to... to what? Even today we hunt them. How I wish we did not. La-la-la... perhaps the man who killed those two enormous Hawksbills decades ago was hungry. Perhaps his children were hungry. I shall not presume to judge him. Nor will I destroy the evidence of his kill. The shells are beautiful; ineffably sad, but beautiful. Would I buy the shell of a turtle today? No. Would I permit a child to buy one? No. But mine are old and beautiful and fragile and sad and I will not destroy or hide them.

Twenty-three Ants

Twenty-three ants have come to drink
From drops of tea in my kitchen sink,
One hundred and thirty-eight legs to raise
Their armoured bodies above the glaze.

Twenty-four thousand compound eyes
To scout terrain where danger lies,
As forty-six antennae taste
The air while mouths suck sugared waste.

And half in wonder — and half amused,
My neat-and-tidy parts confused,
My brain commands a vengeful thumb—
A man-God's whim: no flood shall come!

AUGUST, 2007

Unwanted Miracle

The filter in the pond is packed with snails,
I scoop them out and plop them by a fern.
The older goldfish sneer and flick their tails:
As soon as God has left, the snails return.

FEBRUARY, 2004

'The storm has passed...'

The faintest hint, not far away,
Of azure blue in iron grey,
A dragon's tantrum turned to tears
In distant rumbling no one hears;

The spindrift settles to its source
As sky and sea renew divorce,
As blank Horizon snaps his rule
To right the world for beast and fool;

And men creep out with wary eyes
To scan the still uncertain skies.
The sun peeps out on ragged wings:
The storm has passed—
                          a small bird sings.

190

AUGUST, 2007

'We've a tree here on Mustique...'

We've a tree here on Mustique, growing in the middle of the street.
  It reads 'Keep Left'. While this tree stands, unconscious of its role,
(A green canary in a mine of gold and waxed Versace feet)
  The chances are, if chance there is, our island may retain its soul.

JANUARY, 2005

'We are not who we think we are...'

We are not who we think we are,
    Our lives slide slant as blood runs true,
Lost estuaries from near and far,
    Debris of me, the silt of you.

We are not what the wise have said,
    Our words the stolen scrawl of scribes,
The alphabets of gods long dead,
    The coded scrolls of vanished tribes.

We are not where we thought to be—
    Nor ever stood in Eden's shade,
Memory gilds the stricken tree,
    And decks with bloom a barren glade.

APRIL, 2004

Where the Rain Comes From in Senegal

Each drop of rain was once a soul in sin,
    Hell's demons spit them out in lieu of rent;
They drum upon our roofs of mud and tin,
    Reminding unbelievers to repent!

But what of those who lived by His commands
    And loved the Lord and never told a lie?
God's plan was they should water desert sands
    As angels' tears— but angels never cry.

JULY, 2003

Will is Dead

To the imperishable glory
of William Shakespeare

Abandoned vineyards leave but little trace;
Untrodden cellars leach away their joys;
Our dialect — the glory of our race —
Breeds noble rot that sickens and destroys,
A feeble sediment to salt the bread
Of half a hundred tongues. Let it be so.
To live there must be will, yet Will is dead;
Our vintages decline; our stock is low.

No scholar I. Perhaps I but mistake
The rap of master vintners at the door —
A pretty thought! But, oh, this stuff we make
Is residue of wine too long in store,
And in my heart I fear the muse has fled.
Our words are watered wine;
                        and Will is dead.

AUGUST, 2002

After the Tiff

My dear, you appear to sport
A particle on your lip,
(A scrap of ventricle) hung skew-whiff,
Which accidentally caught
When little white teeth did rip
My heart to shreds. Come, let's forget the tiff—
Beg pardon and relief,
Now here's my handkerchief.

MARCH, 2006

'World is lunatic...'

World is lunatic, his grass as crazed
As any counterfeit Napoleon
Found raving in his cell — each blade amazed
To hear their cousin reeds' aeolian
Rebellion, whispering in minor key
Across the steppe: *'Join us and learn to sing,*
Mute fodder for the herds— cry mutiny!
Join us!' As mad as any warring king
Who builds himself a cage to call a throne.
World's bones, beneath unquiet seas, thrust up
New monuments of twisted rock and stone,
His mountain lakes a mocking victor's cup
To toast the Sky in sulphur and in flame.
And Sky himself, then not to be outdone,
Brings ruin to those puny cairns of fame
Erected by some long forgotten son
Of long forgotten tribes with storm and wrack,
The patient, endless scrape of wind and sand,
Hard rains and hail to flood such bric-a-brac
Down, down to the sea— and so reclaim the land.

World is lunatic, demented in his bliss;
Even the stars — though pitiless — know this.

MARCH, 2005

Sokal's Lake

Lines to mark the
10th anniversary of
Alan Sokal's paper.

The tyranny of twaddle marches on,
And roots of minus one bring joys to fools—
After many a howler dies the swan:
In Sokal's lake of *jouissance*— po-mo rules!

'The lake is solid ground...' 'The lake is dead...'
'There never was a lake... it's just a word...'
'All lakes are in the mind,' the bishop said,
Discretely edging further from the bird.

As flattery debases what it loathes
So swans of truth may smash illusion's oar—
The Emperors of po-mo seek new clothes,
With Johnson's rock between them
                              — and the shore.

AUGUST, 2006

The 'Sokal Affair' was a debunking in 1996 of the fashionable nonsense claimed as holy writ on college campuses throughout the Western world by 'po-mo' (post-modernist) lecturers and theorists. Their claim was (still is) that fact and fiction is indistinguishable. That 'context' is all and there can be no legitimacy for any value-judgement at all. Some professors went so far as to mark down papers from students containing the word 'reality' without quotation marks. To Alan Sokal, a professor of physics at New York University, this was a betrayal of the Enlightenment and a slippery slope back to medievalism. So he wrote a spoof article, packed with the pseudo-scientific drivel and hocus-pocus in which so much po-mo theory loves to cloak itself, and submitted it to 'Social Text', the leading American Journal of post-modern 'cultural studies'. His article was called 'Transgressing the Boundaries: Toward a Transformative Hermeneutics of Quantum Gravity'. Could the august professors on the editorial board of this learned journal possible buy the gibberish that Sokal had sent them unsolicited? Of course they could, because it pandered to their sense of self-importance while bolstering their fruit-cake theories. They published it without altering a word. The rest as they say, is history. No matter what post-modernists now claim in their revisionist histories of the Sokal affair, the professor's parody struck a mortal blow against the growing hegemony of po-mo 'little Hitlers' in academic circles. Happy anniversary, professor!

The 'bishop' in the second stanza is Bishop George Berkeley, an 18th century philosopher and proto-'po-mo' who argued in a sermon against the existence of matter. James Boswell remarked to Samuel Johnson that, though ridiculous, it was impossible to refute the Bishop's argument. Johnson famously answered, striking his foot with mighty force against a large stone: 'I refute it thus!'

'Grief seeks Loss...'

Grief seeks Loss —
     and moves in, uninvited,
Maggot-like,
     it hollows out a core;
Dipped in Guilt
     a sepulchre is whited,
Filled with Pain
     a residence is built;
Bricked with Fear
     and shuttered up with hating,
Dark and drear
     the empty rooms above,
Sealed within,
     Grief settles down to waiting;
Late, so late!
     arrives the bailiff, Love.

MARCH, 2006

Our Neighbours

'Of fur and feather, scale and shell,
Those neighbours we consign to hell...'

They use no jails, except those built by men,
    No management, no coin, no entourage;
They rest content, while we must stalk the world,
    Our so-called sentience, mere camouflage.
We lack their speed, their balance and their sight;
    The skill of merely being what we are
Has long been lost to us. But not to them!
    They make community, but pass no jar
Among themselves to drown the gods of wrath.
    They do no ill, far less do they conspire
To pox the world with gulags — or with slaves;
    Not one has ever sought a man for hire.

They foul no earth, they scorch no forest black;
    And if they kill, they feed upon the lame.
They scourge no lakes, nor fill the sea with wrack.
    They mate beneath the sun and not in shame;
They bind the world — mysterious, in such ways
    As we have yet to learn or understand.
They dig no graves, nor mines. They scar no hills.
    They bear no judas gifts to blight the land.
They know no guilt — nor have they reason to.
    If courtesy could salvage men's despite,
Have they not paid due ransom? Search your heart:
    Their beauty is a child's chief delight.

JANUARY, 2004

So here we are at the end of my book, and here is a bonus poem to bring the total to a round hundred in *Island of Dreams*. (You knew that would happen, gentle reader; didn't you?) I make no excuse for choosing another hymn of praise to Patsy Fisher. The rich and the famous certainly make life interesting on Mustique. And the hard work of The Mustique Company's staff, along with many others, makes it possible. But Patsy Fisher (and people like her) make it a *joy!*

Someone is Missing

(for Patsy Fisher 1932 - 2006)

Someone is missing— a crafter of quiet,
A beacon of love in the midst of riot;

Someone whose laughter scattered the thunder,
Someone who saw through eyes of wonder;

Someone who reckoned hate a blindness,
Someone who smothered fault with kindness;

Someone who wore her learning lightly,
Someone whose gentleness chided us slightly;

Someone who fashioned her heart a palace,
Someone whose innocence walled out malice;

Someone who harnessed hurt to healing,
Someone who knew just how you were feeling;

Someone whose painterly eye saw through you,
Someone who loved you before she knew you;

Someone who never called in her marker:
Someone is missing. And life is darker.

DECEMBER, 2006

Index

211

Acknowledgements

Many people assisted with the creation of this book. Some gave days of their time. Some merely made a brilliant suggestion for the subject of a poem or the location of a rare plant or tree on Mustique.

They include: Rebecca Jezzard, the designer of *Island of Dreams*; Bill Sanderson for his illustrations of Patsy Fisher, Arne Hasselqvist and Subha Chinnayan; Alex Watson for the photograph on page 47; The Mustique Company and its hard working personnel; Sheneal Liverpool and Melissa Joseph at The Mustique Community Library; several Departments of the Government of St. Vincent & the Grenadines; the Prime Minister's Office of St. Vincent & the Grenadines; the Governor General's Office of St. Vincent & the Grenadines; the staff of Dennis Publishing in the UK; Toby Fisher; Lana James; Don and Sue Atyeo; the staff (and especially the gardeners) of Mandalay House, Shogun House and many other houses and parts of Mustique; Marie-France Demolis and other homeowners across the island; the staff, owners and managers of many commercial businesses and retail outlets on Mustique; the personal staff of my private office in London; George Taylor and Dan Gable for their talented help on the audio CD; Caroline Rush for seeing the book through each tranche of its gestation and, lastly, my poetry editor, Simon Rae and reader, Moni Mannings.

Sybil Sparkes and I are most grateful to you all.